XTREME INSECTS
Beetles

BY S.L. HAMILTON

A&D Xtreme
An imprint of Abdo Publishing | www.abdopublishing.com

Visit us at
www.abdopublishing.com

Published by Abdo Publishing Company, a division of ABDO, PO Box 398166, Minneapolis, MN 55439. Copyright ©2015 by Abdo Consulting Group, Inc. International copyrights reserved in all countries. No part of this book may be reproduced in any form without written permission from the publisher. A&D Xtreme™ is a trademark and logo of Abdo Publishing Company.

Printed in the United States of America, North Mankato, Minnesota.
102014
012015

PRINTED ON RECYCLED PAPER

Editor: John Hamilton
Graphic Design: Sue Hamilton
Cover Design: Sue Hamilton
Cover Photo: Corbis
Interior Photos: Alberta Sustainable Resource Development-pg 25 (bottom left); AP-pg 24 (bottom right); Corbis-pgs 18-19 & 20-21; Igor Siwanowicz-pg 13 (inset); iStock-pgs 1, 2-3, 6, 7, 12-13, 26, 28 (inset), 30-31 & 32; Minden Pictures-pgs 4-5, 10-11 & 16-17; Purdue University Dept of Entomology/John Obermeyer-pg 24 (top); Science Source-pgs 8-9, 14-15, 22, 23, 27 & 28-29; Susan Tooker-pg 19 (inset), U.S. Customs and Border Protection-pg 15 (inset); University of Colorado Boulder/Jeffry Mitton-pg 25 (top); University of Northern British Columbia/Dezene Huber-pg 25 (bottom right); Virginia Polytechnic Institute and State University/Eric R. Day-pg 24 (bottom left).

Websites
To learn more about Xtreme Insects, visit booklinks.abdopublishing.com. These links are routinely monitored and updated to provide the most current information available.

Library of Congress Control Number: 2014944882
Cataloging-in-Publication Data
Hamilton, S.L.
  Beetles / S.L. Hamilton.
    p. cm. -- (Xtreme insects)
ISBN 978-1-62403-688-0 (lib. bdg.)
Includes index.
1. Beetles--Juvenile literature.   I. Title.
595.76--dc23

2014944882

Contents

Beetles

Beetles are one of the most successful living creatures on Earth. About 350,000 beetle species are known to science, but there are likely thousands more. These amazing insects have survived on Earth for more than 270 million years. They have adapted to nearly every environment in the world.

XTREME FACT – Beetles are the Earth's largest group of animals. They represent one-fifth of all known living organisms.

Body Parts

Beetles have six legs and three distinct body parts: head, thorax, and abdomen. They belong to the order coleoptera, which means "sheath wings." Their flying wings are covered by a protective second pair of wings called the elytra.

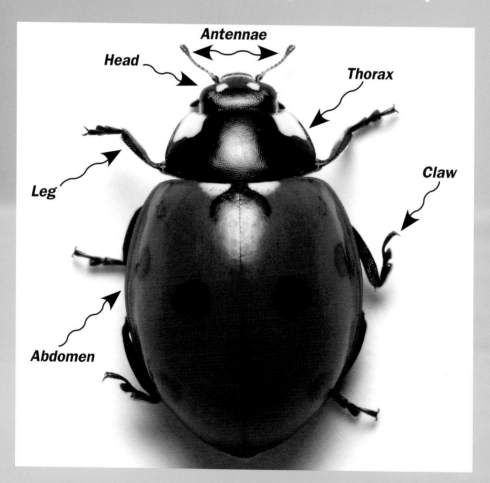

Antennae

Head

Thorax

Leg

Claw

Abdomen

XTREME FACT – Beetles vary from each other in their antenna structure, number of foot segments, connections between body parts, and the number of wings they have.

Flying Wings

Elytra

Titan Beetle

The enormous titan beetle is found in the rain forests of South America. It can grow to 7 inches (18 cm) in length. When threatened, the titan beetle emits a loud warning hiss.

To defend themselves, male titan beetles have rows of sharp spines on their legs. Both males and females have powerful jaws and sharp mandibles that can tear into flesh.

Hercules Beetle

The tough Hercules beetle is the largest type of rhinoceros beetle. It is super strong, able to carry 850 times its own weight. If a human could do that, it would be like lifting a 65-ton (59-metric ton) armored tank.

The Hercules beetle is found on every continent except Antarctica. It is not only strong, it is also one of the longest beetles. It may reach lengths as long as 17.5 inches (44 cm). About half its length is taken up by its enormous horns. The horns are used to drive away other male beetles from a female. They are also used to dig into leaves and dirt to help create a hiding place from predators.

XTREME FACT – The Hercules beetle is named after the ancient Greek hero who possesses super strength.

Tiger Beetle

Tiger beetles are the Olympic runners of the beetle world. The fastest tiger beetle moves at a rate of 5.6 miles per hour (9 kph). That's equal to a human running at 480 miles per hour (772 kph).

Tiger beetles have large curved mandibles. They are aggressive hunters and can easily run down other insects for food.

XTREME FACT – Tiger beetles run so fast their vision blurs. Their eyes do not have time to form an image. They must stop for a moment, look, then run again. They point their antennae in front to help keep themselves from running into things.

Ironclad Beetle

Some beetles have such tough exoskeletons that they are considered to be "armored." The ironclad beetle's exoskeleton is thick. It seems as strong as iron, which gives the beetle its name. An ironclad beetle can be stepped on by a human and remain unhurt.

Ironclad beetles are found in dry areas such as the American Southwest and Mexico. These beetles defend themselves by playing dead. This action is known as thanatosis. The beetles freeze when touched or disturbed.

XTREME FACT –
Because of their tough exoskeleton and their ability to play dead, ironclad beetles are sometimes decorated with gold chains and gems and sold as "living jewelry" for people to wear.

Bombardier Beetle

A bombardier beetle is armed with its own chemical weaponry. When threatened, two separate liquids pour into a single storage chamber inside the beetle. If the bombardier beetle is attacked, the solutions move into a smaller explosion chamber. Heat is created by additional chemicals. In an instant, the bombardier beetle aims and shoots boiling-hot gas from its backside.

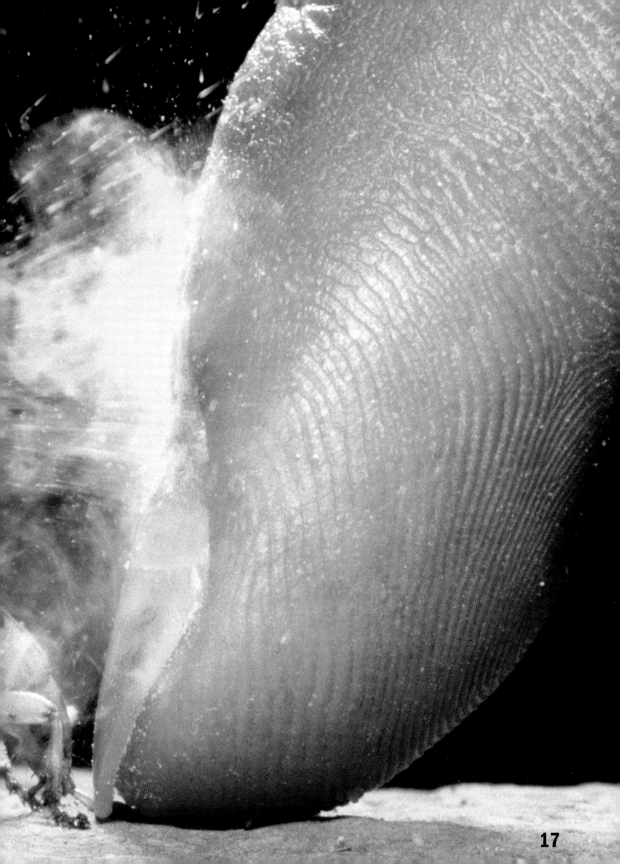

Jewel Beetle

Jewel beetles are beautiful. Some have bright, iridescent colors. They are one of the largest groups of beetles, with more than 15,000 species. Many jewel beetles's elytra, or wing coverings, are used to create jewelry and other decorations.

A necklace made of jewel beetle elytra.

Firefly or Lightning Bug

Some beetles give off light. The most well-known is the firefly, or lightning bug. A chemical reaction within a firefly's body makes an organ on its abdomen flash. Males flash to attract the attention of females. Females flash back when they are interested. Some people collect the flashing fireflies in a jar and use them as a natural light source.

Ladybugs

Some beetles are helpful to humans. Ladybird beetles, more commonly known as ladybugs or seven-spot bugs, are a gardener's best friend. These popular beetles eat aphids, mites, mealybugs, and other small pests that damage and kill plants and flowers.

Ground Beetles

Ground beetles eat nearly anything that moves near them. Since they do not climb, these helpful beetles make their lunch from what they find on the ground. This includes crop-damaging pests such as aphids, asparagus beetles, cabbage worms, Colorado potato beetles, and corn earworms.

Emerald Ash Borer

Some beetles are destructive. Emerald ash borers and mountain pine beetles gnaw into ash and pine trees and lay their eggs.

Mountain Pine Beetle

When emerald ash borer and mountain pine beetle larvae hatch, they start munching on the tree. These beetles kill millions of trees every year.

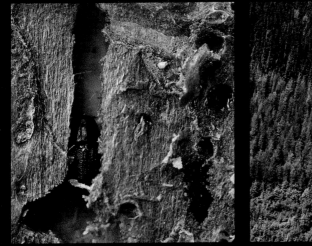

Colorado Potato Beetle

The Colorado potato beetle and its larvae eat the leaves of potatoes, tomatoes, peppers, and eggplants. This destroys the plants. At the end of the growing season, the young bury themselves in the soil and do it all again the following year.

XTREME FACT – A single female potato beetle may lay as many as 800 eggs. This makes them difficult to kill off.

Weevils

Weevils are beetles with a long snout and chewing mouthparts at the end. Many weevils eat one kind of plant, and are named after it. The boll weevil eats cotton flowers and seed pods, or bolls. There are also rice, flour, wheat, bean, and cowpea weevils that devour those plants. Weevils can destroy entire fields of crops.

Boll Weevil

XTREME FACT –
There are more species of weevils than any other group of beetles.

Can You Eat Them?

Beetles are eaten in eighty percent of the world. They are an excellent source of protein. Beetles are easy to find and collect. Beetle larvae, the worm-like stage of young beetles, are eaten in many areas around the world.

XTREME FACT– Many people do not like eating beetles because biting down on the exoskeleton makes a yucky "pop" when it breaks.

Glossary

APHID
A small bug that feeds on the sap in plants. Aphids reproduce quickly and in large numbers, and if not stopped, will severely damage or kill the plants on which they live.

ELYTRA
The outer coverings that protect a beetle's wings.

EXOSKELETON
The hard outer surface that frames a beetle's body. The exoskeleton provides support and protection for the beetle.

IRIDESCENT
Bright colors that seem to glow. Some may appear to change color when viewed from different angles.

IRON
A gray metal known for its strength.

LARVA
A newly hatched insect, usually wormlike in shape, that has yet to change into its adult form.

MANDIBLES
Strong, beak-like mouth organs that are used for grabbing and biting food.

PREDATOR
A creature that feeds on other creatures.

SPECIES
A group of living things that have similar looks and behaviors, but are not identical. They are often called by a similar name. For example, there are more than 350,000 species of beetles.

THANATOSIS
When an insect, such as a beetle, feels threatened and freezes in place. When the beetle is in a state of thanatosis, it looks as though it is dead. The beetle hopes whatever is disturbing it leaves it alone.

THORAX
The middle section of an insect's body, between the head and the abdomen.

Index

DATE DUE

			PRINTED IN U.S.A